A Midsu...
Night's Dream

WRITTEN
BY
WILLIAM SHAKESPEARE

ADAPTED
BY
L. HENRY DOWELL

BLACK BOX THEATRE PUBLISHING

<u>CAST</u>

Theseus
Hippolyta
Egeus
Demetrius
Hermia
Lysander
Helena
Bottom
Flute
Quince
Snout
Snuggles the Circus Midget
Starveling
Puck
Fairy
Oberon
Titania
Cobweb
Moth
Mustardseed
Peaseblossom
The Little Indian Boy
Philostrate

A Midsummer Night's Dream

SCENE 1

THESEUS, HIPPOLYTA and
PHILOSTRATE enter.

THESEUS

Now, fair Hippolyta, our wedding hour draws apace. Four
happy days bring in another moon, but Oh, methinks how
slow this old moon wanes! She lingers my desires like to a
step-mother or a wealthy widow, long withering out a young
man's revenue.

HIPPOLYTA

Four days will quickly steep themselves in night, four nights
will quickly dream away the time. And then the moon, like to
a silver bow new bent in heaven, shall behold the night of our
celebrations.

THESEUS

Go, Philostrate. Stir up the Athenian youth to merriments.
Awake the pert and nimble spirit of mirth, turn melancholy
forth to funerals. The pale companion is not for our pomp.
Hippolyta, I wooed thee with my sword, and won thy love by
defeating thee. But I will wed thee in another manner. With
pomp, with triumph, and with reveling.

PHILOSTRATE exits. EGEUS, HERMIA,
LYSANDER and DEMETRIUS enter.

EGEUS

Happy be Theseus, our renowned Duke!

THESEUS

Thanks, good Egeus. What's the news with thee?

EGEUS

Full of vexations come I, with complaint against my child,
my daughter Hermia. Stand forth, Demetrius.

(DEMETRIUS steps forward.)

My noble lord, this man hath my consent to marry her. Stand
forth, Lysander.

(LYSANDER steps forward.)

And, my gracious Duke, this man hath bewitched the bosom
of my child.

(To LYSANDER.)

With cunning hast thou filched my daughter's heart, turned
her obedience, which is due to me, to stubborn harshness.

(To THESEUS.)

And, my gracious Duke, be it so she will not here before your
Grace consent to marry with Demetrius, I beg the ancient
privilege of Athens, as she is mine, I may dispose of her,
which shall be either to marry this gentleman, or to her death,
according to our law immediately provided in that case.

THESEUS

What say you, Hermia? Demetrius is a worthy gentleman.

HERMIA

So is Lysander.

THESEUS

In himself he is, but in this kind, wanting your father's voice,
Demetrius must be held the worthier.

HERMIA

I would my father looked but with my eyes.

THESEUS

Rather your eyes, must with his judgment look.

HERMIA

I do entreat your Grace to pardon me. I know not by what
power I am made bold, nor how it may concern my modesty
in such a presence here to plead my thought, but I beseech
your Grace, that I may know the worst that may befall me in
this case, if I refuse to wed Demetrius.

THESEUS

Either to die the death, or have no further contact with men!

HERMIA

So will I grow, so live, so die, my lord, before I will marry a
man I do not love!

THESEUS

Take time to pause, and by the next new moon, my wedding
day, upon that day either prepare to die for disobedience to
your father's will, or else to wed Demetrius.

DEMETRIUS

Relent, sweet Hermia, and Lysander, yield thy crazed title to
my certain right.

LYSANDER

You have her father's love, Demetrius. Let me have
Hermia's. Why don't you marry him?

> DEMETRIUS and EGEUS look at EACH
> OTHER, disgusted.

EGEUS

Scornful Lysander! True, he hath my love and what is mine
my love shall render him. And she is mine, and all my right
of her, I do give unto Demetrius.

LYSANDER

I am, my Lord, as well derived as he, as well possessed, and my love is more than his. He courted old Nedar's daughter, Helena, and she is madly in love with him.

THESEUS

I must confess that I have heard as much. Demetrius. Egeus. Come with me. I wish to speak to you both.

EGEUS

With duty and desire, we follow you.

ALL exit, except HERMIA and
LYSANDER

LYSANDER

How now, my love? Why is your cheek so pale? How chance the roses there do fade so fast?

HERMIA

Belike for want of rain, which I could well beteem them from the tempest of my eyes.

LYSANDER

Oh, me! For aught that I could ever read, could ever hear by tale or history, the course of true love never did run smooth. But either it was different in blood...

HERMIA

O cross! Too high to be enthralled to low.

LYSANDER

Or else ill-matched, in respect of years...

HERMIA

O spite! Too old to be engaged to young.

LYSANDER
Or else it stood upon the choice of friends...

HERMIA
How awful! To choose love through another's eyes.

LYSANDER
Listen to me, Hermia. I have a widowed aunt. A dowager of
great revenue, and she hath no child, and respects me as her
only son. Her house is about twenty miles from Athens
There, gentle Hermia, may I marry thee.

HERMIA
My good Lysander, I promise to meet you tomorrow at the
appointed place.

LYSANDER
Keep promise, love. Look, here comes Helena.

HELENA enters.

HERMIA
God speed, fair Helena! Whither away?

HELENA
Call you me "fair"? That "fair" again unsay! Demetrius loves
your fair. Oh happy fair! Sickness is catching, oh, were favor
so! Yours would I catch, fair Hermia, ere I go. My ear should
catch you voice, my eye your eye. My tongue should catch
your tongue's sweet melody. Were all the world mine,
Demetrius being bated, the rest I'll give to be to you
translated. Oh, teach me how you look and with what art you
sway the motion of Demetrius' heart!

HERMIA
I frown upon him, yet he loves me still.

HELENA

Oh, that your frowns would teach my smiles such skill!

HERMIA

I give him curses, yet he gives me love.

HELENA

Oh, that my prayers could such affection move!

HERMIA

The more I hate, the more he follows me.

HELENA

The more I love, the more he hateth me.

HERMIA

His folly, Helena, is no fault of mine.

HELENA

None but your beauty, would that fault were mine!

HERMIA

Take comfort. He no more shall see my face. Lysander and myself will fly this place.

LYSANDER

Helen, we'll confide in you. Tomorrow night, when the moon sees her reflection in the sea, and dew falls on the grass, just the right time for eloping lovers, we plan to steal through the gates of Athens.

HERMIA

And in the wood, where you and I often used to lie on beds of pale primroses, confiding our secrets to each other, Lysander and I will meet. We'll turn our backs on Athens and seek new friends and the companionship of strangers. Farewell, sweet playfellow! Pray for us, and may good luck grant you your Demetrius. Keep your promise, Lysander. We must deny ourselves the joy of seeing each other till midnight tomorrow.

HERMIA exits.

LYSANDER

I will, my Hermia. Helena, adieu. As you on him, Demetrius dote on you!

LYSANDER exits.

HELENA

How happy some o'er other some can be! Through Athens I am thought as fair as she. But what of that? Demetrius thinks not so. He will not know what all be he do know. And as he errs, doting on Hermia's eyes, so I, admiring of his qualities. Things base and vile, holding no quantity, Love can transpose to form and dignity. Love looks not with the eyes, but with the mind, and therefore is winged Cupid painted blind. Nor hath Love's mind of any judgment taste. Before Demetrius looked on Hermia's eyes, he hailed down oaths that he was only mine. And when this hail some heat from Hermia felt, so he dissolved and the showers of oaths did melt. I will go tell him of fair Hermia's flight, then to the wood will he tomorrow night pursue her. And for this intelligence, if I have thanks, it is a dear expense. But herein mean I to enrich my pain, to have his sight thither, and back again.

LIGHTS: BLACKOUT.

SCENE 2

QUINCE, SNUGGLES, BOTTOM,
FLUTE, SNOUT, and STARVELING enter.

QUINCE
Is all our company here?

BOTTOM
You were best to call them generally, man by man, according
to the script.

QUINCE
Here is the scroll of every man's name, which is thought fit,
through all Athens, to play in our interlude before the Duke
and the Duchess on his wedding day at night.

BOTTOM
First, good Peter Quince, say what the play treats on. Then
read the names of the actors, and so grow to a point.

QUINCE
Marry, our play is "The Most Lamentable Comedy and Most
Cruel Death of Pyramus and Thisbe".

BOTTOM
A very good piece of work, I assure you, and a merry. Now,
good Peter Quince, call forth your actors by the scroll.
        (ALL crowd in.)
Masters, spread yourselves.
        (ALL spread out.)

QUINCE
Answer as I call you. Nick Bottom, the weaver?

BOTTOM
Ready. Name what part I am for, and proceed.

QUINCE
You, Nick Bottom, are set down for Pyramus.

BOTTOM
What is Pyramus? A lover or a tyrant?

QUINCE
A lover, that kills himself most gallant for love.

BOTTOM
That will ask some tears in the true performing of it. If I do it,
let the audience look to their eyes. I will move storms, I will
condole in some measure. Yet, my chief humor is for a
tyrant. I could play Hercules rarely, or a part to tear a cat in,
to make all split:

The raging rocks, And shivering shocks,
Shall break the locks of prison gates.
And Phibbus' car shall shine from far
and make and mar the foolish fates.

This was lofty! This is Hercules's vein, a tyrant's vein. A
lover is more condoling. Now name the rest of the players.

QUINCE
Francis Flute, the bellows-mender?

FLUTE
Here, Peter Quince.

QUINCE
Flute, you must take Thisbe on you.

FLUTE
What is Thisbe? A wandering knight?

QUINCE
It is the lady that Pyramus must love.

FLUTE

Nay, faith, let not me play a woman. I have a beard coming!

ALL

(Gathering around FLUTE.)
Where? Do you see any hair? I don't. Etc.

QUINCE

That's all one, you shall play it in a mask, and you may speak
as small as you will.

BOTTOM

As I may hide my face, let me play Thisbe too! I'll speak in a
monstrous little voice.
      (Speaks in a girly voice.)
"Thisne, Thisne." "Ah Pyramus, my lover dear! Thy Thisbe
dear, and lady dear!"

QUINCE

No, no, you must play Pyramus and Flute, you Thisbe.

BOTTOM

Well, proceed.

QUINCE

Robin Starveling, the tailor?

STARVELING

Here, Peter Quince.

QUINCE

Robin Starveling, you must play Thisbe's mother. Tom
Snout, the Tinker?

SNOUT

Here, Peter Quince.

QUINCE

You are Pyramus' father. Myself, Thisbe's father. Snuggles the Circus Midget, you have the lion's part, and I hope here is a play fitted.

SNUGGLES

Have you the lion's part written? Pray you, if it be, give it to me, for I am slow of study.

QUINCE

You can make it up, for it is nothing but roaring.

BOTTOM

Let me play the lion too! I will roar that I will do any man's heart good to hear me. I will roar so that I will make the Duke say, "Let him roar again! Let him roar again!"

QUINCE

And you should do it too terribly and you would frighten the Duchess and the ladies! Then they would shriek and that were enough to hang us all.

ALL agree. Someone says "Etc."

BOTTOM

I grant you friends, if you should frighten the ladies out of their wits, they would have no more discretion but to hang us. But I will aggravate my voice so, that I will roar you as gently as any sucking dove. I will roar you as t'were any nightingale. Roawr. Roawr.

QUINCE

You can play no part but Pyramus! Pyramus is a sweet faced man, a proper man as one shall see in a summer's day. A most lovely, gentleman-like man. Therefore you must needs play Pyramus.

BOTTOM

Well...I will undertake it. What beard were I best to play it in?

QUINCE

Why, what you will.

BOTTOM

I will discharge in either your straw-colored beard, your orange-tawny beard, your purple-in-grain beard, or your French-crown-colored beard, your perfect yellow.

QUINCE

Some of your French crowns have no hair at all!

ALL laugh. "He made a French joke!"

QUINCE

And then you would play bare-faced. But, masters, here are you parts, and I am to entreat you, request you, and desire you to learn them by tomorrow night. Meet me in the palace wood, a mile without the town by moonlight. There we will rehearse, for if we meet in the city, we shall be dogged with company and our devices known. In the mean time, I will draw a bill of properties, such as our play wants. I pray you, fail me not!

BOTTOM

We will meet and there we may rehearse most obscenely and courageously. Take pains, be perfect! Adieu!

QUINCE

At the Duke's oak we meet.

BOTTOM

Right! Be there or be square!

LIGHTS: BLACKOUT.

SCENE 3

A FAIRY, and PUCK enter from opposite
sides.

PUCK

How now, spirit! Whither wander you?

FAIRY

Over hill, over dale, through bush, through brier, over park,
over pale, through flood, through fire, I do wander
everywhere. Swifter than the moon's sphere and I serve the
fairy queen, to dew her orbs upon the green. The cowslips tall
her pensioners be, in their gold coats spots you see. Those be
rubies, fairy favors, in those freckles live their savors. I must
go seek some dewdrops here and hang a pearl in every
cowslip's ear. Farewell, thou lob of spirits, I'll be gone. Our
Queen and all our elves come here anon.

PUCK

The King doth keep his revels here tonight. Take heed the
Queen come not within his sight. For Oberon is passing fell
and wrath, because that she as her attendant hath a lovely
boy, stolen from an Indian King. She never had so sweet a
changeling. And jealous Oberon would have the child!

FAIRY

Either I mistake your shape and making quite, or else you are
that shrewd and knavish sprite called Robin Goodfellow. Are
you not he?

PUCK

That's me alright!
          (Woody Woodpecker laugh.)
But stand aside, Fairy! Here comes Oberon.

FAIRY

And here comes my mistress. Would that he were gone!

OBERON enters from one side, TITANIA
and her FAIRIES from the other.

OBERON
Ill met by moonlight, proud Titania.

TITANIA
What, jealous Oberon! Fairies, skip hence.

OBERON
Not so fast, Lady! Am I not thy husband?

TITANIA
Then I must be thy lady.

OBERON
Why should Titania cross her Oberon? I do but beg a little
Indian Boy, to be my henchman.

TITANIA
Set your heart at rest. The fairy land buys not the child of me.
His mother was a votaress of my order, and in the spiced
Indian air by night, full often hath she gossiped by my side.
But she, being mortal, died in childbirth and for her sake I am
bringing up her boy. And for her sake, I won't part with him.

OBERON
How long within this wood intend you stay?

TITANIA
Perchance till after Theseus' wedding-day. If you will
patiently dance in our round and see our moonlight revels, go
with us. If not, shun me, and I will spare your haunts.

OBERON
Give me that boy, and I will go with thee.

TITANIA

Not for thy fairy kingdom. Fairies, away! We shall chide
downright, if I longer stay.

TITANIA and FAIRIES exit.

OBERON

Well, go thy way! You won't leave this grove till I've made
you suffer for this insult! My gentle Puck, come hither. Do
you remember the time when I sat on a jutting rock and heard
a mermaid on a dolphin's back, singing with such sweetness
and harmony that the rough sea grew calm and certain stars
shot madly out of their orbits on hearing the mermaid's
music?

PUCK

I remember.

OBERON

That selfsame time I saw armed Cupid, though you could not,
flying between the cold moon and the earth. He took true aim
at a chaste queen ruling a western island. He fired an arrow
of love smartly from his bow with enough force to pierce a
hundred thousand hearts. The pure beams of the pale moon
stopped young Cupid's passionate arrow. So, she passed on,
thinking her maidenly thoughts, unconcerned with love. But I
took note of where Cupid's arrow fell. It fell upon a little
western flower, white originally, now purple with love's
wound. Maidens call it "love-in-idleness"; the pansy. Fetch
me that flower. I showed it to you once. If its juice is laid on
sleeping eyelids, the man or woman is made to fall madly in
love with the next creature seen. Fetch me this flower, and
come back again before a giant whale can swim three miles.

PUCK

I'll encircle the earth in forty minutes!
        (As Speedy Gonzales.)
Andale! Andale! Arriba! Arriba!

PUCK exits.

OBERON

Having once this juice, I'll watch Titania when she is asleep, and drop the liquor of it in her eyes. The next thing then, she waking looks upon, be it on lion, bear, wolf, bull, meddling monkey, or on busy ape, she shall pursue it with the soul of love. And ere I take this charm from off her sight, as I can take it with another herb, I'll make her render up the boy to me. But who comes here? I am invisible and I will overhear their conference.

DEMETRIUS and HELENA enter.

DEMETRIUS

I love thee not, therefore pursue me not. Get thee gone, and follow me no more!

HELENA

You draw me, you hard-hearted adamant. But yet you draw not iron, for my heart is true as steel. Leave you your power to draw, and I shall have no power to follow you.

DEMETRIUS

Do I entice you? Do I speak you fair? Or, rather, do I not in plainest truth tell you, I do not, and cannot love you?

HELENA

And even for that do I love you the more. I am your spaniel and, Demetrius, the more you beat me, I will fawn on you. Use me but as your spaniel, spurn me, strike me, neglect me, lose me. Only give me leave, unworthy as I am, to follow you. What worser place can I beg in your love, and yet a place of high respect with me, than to be used as you use your dog?

DEMETRIUS

Sit Ubu, sit! Tempt not too much the hatred of my spirit, for I am sick when I do look on thee.

HELENA

And I am sick when I look not on you.

DEMETRIUS

You do impeach your modesty too much! I'll run from thee and hide me in the brakes, and leave thee to the mercy of wild beasts.

HELENA

The wildest hath not such a heart as you. Run where you will, the story shall be changed! The dove pursues the griffin. The mild deer makes speed to catch the tiger, bootless speed, when cowardice pursues and valor flies.

DEMETRIUS

I will not stay thy questions. Let me go! Or, if thou follow me, do not believe but I shall do thee mischief in the wood.

HELENA

Ay, in the temple, in the town, the field, you do me mischief. Fie, Demetrius! Your wrongs do set a scandal on me! We cannot fight for love, as men may do. We should be wooed and were not made to woo.

DEMETRIUS exits.

HELENA

I'll follow you and find happiness in my misery. I'll die upon the hand I love so well.

HELENA exits, chasing after DEMETRIUS.

OBERON

Fare thee well, nymph. Ere he do leave this grove, thou shalt
fly him and he shall seek thy love.

PUCK enters dressed as delivery man.

OBERON

Hast thou the flower there, welcome wanderer?

PUCK

Ay, there it is.

OBERON

Give it to me, please. I know where Titania sleeps tonight.
And with the juice of this, I'll streak her eyes. You take some
of it, and go searching through this grove. A sweet Athenian
lady is in love with a youth who rejects her. Anoint his eyes,
but do it when the next thing he sees will be the lady. You'll
know the man by the Athenian clothes he is wearing. Do it
carefully, so he'll be more infatuated with her than she with
him. See you meet me again before morning breaks.

PUCK

Don't worry, my lord. Your servant will obey.

LIGHTS: BLACKOUT.

SCENE 4

TITANIA and FAIRIES enter.

TITANIA
Come now! Let's dance in a ring and sing a fairy song.

MUSIC: FAIRIES dance, at end THEY lay
down and sleep. OBERON enters.

OBERON
What you see when you awake, fall in love with, by mistake!
Love and suffer for his sake! Be it lynx, wild cat, bear,
leopard, or boar with bristly hair. Whatever to your eyes
appears, when you awake, its sight endears.
(Pause. Touches HER eyelids with flower.)
Wake when something nasty nears.
(Pauses. Turns to the audience.)
Bwah-ha-ha-ha-ha.

OBERON exits. LYSANDER and
HERMIA enter.

LYSANDER
I have forgot our way. We'll rest here, Hermia, if you think it
good, and tarry for the comfort of the day.

HERMIA
Be it so, Lysander. Find you out a bed, for I upon this bank
will rest my head.

LYSANDER sits close to HER.

LYSANDER
One turf shall serve as pillow for us both. One heart, one bed,
two bosoms and one troth.

HERMIA

Nay, good Lysander. For my sake, my dear, lie further off
yet, do not lie so near.

> (SHE motions for HIM to move away. HE does,
> slightly.)

Gentle friend, in the name of love and good manners, lie
further off, out of common decency. About as far a distance
as would be thought proper between a virtuous bachelor and
a single girl.

> (SHE motions for HIM to lay further off. HE
> moves. SHE motions again. Again, HE moves.
> SHE motions again. HE moves. Finally, SHE is
> satisfied.)

This far apart. Goodnight, sweet friend. May your love never
change as long as you live!

LYSANDER

Amen, amen to that prayer, say I! If I broke faith, I'd deserve
to die. Here's my bed. Sleep peacefully.

HERMIA

With half that wish, the wisher's eyes be pressed.

> THEY sleep. PUCK enters.

PUCK

Through the forest have I gone, but Athenian found I none,
on whose eyes I might approve this flower's force in stirring
love.

> (Spies LYSANDER.)

Night and silence! Who is here? Weeds of Athens he doth
wear. This is he, my master said, despised the Athenian maid.
And here the maiden, sleeping sound, on the dank and dirty
ground. Pretty soul! She durst not lie near this lack-love, this
kill-courtesy. Churl, upon thy eyes I throw all the power this
charm doth owe. When thou wakest, let love forbid sleep his
seat on thy eyelid. So awake when I am gone, for I must now
to Oberon. AWAY! AWAY!

PUCK exits. DEMETRIUS and HELENA enter.

HELENA

Stay, though thou kill me, sweet Demetrius.

DEMETRIUS

I charge thee, hence, and do not haunt me thus.

HELENA

Oh, wilt thou darkling leave me? Do not so.

DEMETRIUS

Stay, on thy peril. I alone will go.

HE exits.

HELENA

Oh, I am out of breath in this fond chase! The more my prayer, the lesser is my grace. Happy is Hermia, wheresoe'er she lies, for she hath blessed and attractive eyes.
(SHE sees LYSANDER.)
But who is here? Lysander! On the ground! Dead? Or asleep? I see no blood. No wound. Lysander if you live, good sir, awake.

LYSANDER

(Awaking. SOUND: BOING!)
HUBBA-HUBBA-HUBBA!!! And run through fire I will for thy sweet sake! Transparent Helena! Nature shows art, that through thy bosom makes me see thy heart. Where is Demetrius? Oh, how fit a word is that vile name to perish on my sword!

HELENA

Do not say so, Lysander. Say not so! What though he love your Hermia? Lord, what though? Yet Hermia still loves you, then be content.

LYSANDER

Content with Hermia! No, I do repent the tedious minutes I with her have spent. Not Hermia, but Helena I love! Who will not trade a raven for a dove? The will of man is by his reason swayed, and reason says you are the worthier maid.

HELENA

Wherefore was I to this keen mockery born? When at your hands did I deserve this scorn? It's not enough, it's not enough, young man, that I did never, no, nor never can, deserve a sweet look from Demetrius' eye, but you must flout my insufficiency? Good troth, you do me wrong, good sooth, you do, in such disdainful manner me to woo! But fare you well, perforce I must confess I thought you lord of more true gentleness. Oh, that a lady, of one man refused, should of another therefore be abused!

HELENA exits.

LYSANDER

She sees not Hermia. Hermia, sleep thou there and never mayst thou come Lysander near! All my powers, address your love and might, to honor Helena and to be her knight.

LYSANDER exits.

HERMIA
(Awaking)

Help me, Lysander, help me! Do thy best to pluck this crawling serpent from my breast! Oh me, for pity! What a dream was here! Lysander, look how I do quake with fear. I thought a serpent ate my heart away, and you sat smiling at his cruel prey.

HERMIA (Cont'd)
(Yelling.)

Lysander! What, removed? Lysander! Lord! What, out of hearing? Gone? No sound, no word? Alack, where are you speak, and if you hear, speak, of all loves! I swoon almost with fear. No? Then I will perceive you all not nigh. Either death or you, I'll find immediately.

HERMIA exits. LIGHTS: BLACKOUT.

SCENE 5

TITANIA, asleep. QUINCE,
SNUGGLES, BOTTOM, FLUTE,
SNOUT, and STARVELING enter.

BOTTOM

Are we all met?

QUINCE

Pat, pat, and here's a marvelous convenient place for our
rehearsal. This green plot shall be our stage, this hawthorn-
brake our tiring-house, and we will do it in action as we will
do it before the Duke.

BOTTOM

Peter Quince!

QUINCE

What sayest thou, bully Bottom?

BOTTOM

There are things in this comedy of Pyramus and Thisbe that
will never please. First, Pyramus must draw a sword to kill
himself, which the ladies cannot abide. How answer you
that?

SNOUT

By our Lady! That's a good point.

STARVELING

I believe we must leave the killing out, when all is done.

BOTTOM

Not a whit. I have a device to make all well. Write me a
prologue, and let the prologue seem to say. We will do no
harm with our swords, and that Pyramus is not killed indeed,
and, for the more better assurance, tell them that I, Pyramus,
am not Pyramus, but Bottom the weaver. This will put them
out of fear.

QUINCE

Well, we will have such a prologue, and it shall be written in
eight and six.

BOTTOM

No, make it two more. Let it be written in eight and eight.

THEY applaud HIS brilliance.

SNOUT

Will not the ladies be afeard of the lion?

STARVELING

I fear it, I promise you.

BOTTOM

Masters, you ought to consider with yourselves. To bring in,
God shield us, a lion among ladies, is a most dreadful thing!
For there is not a more fearful wild-fowl than your lion
living, and we ought to look to it.

SNOUT

Therefore another prologue must tell he is not a lion.

BOTTOM

Nay, you must name his name, and half his face must be seen
through the lion's neck, and he himself must speak through,
saying thus, or to the same defect. "Ladies," or "Fair-ladies I
would wish you," or "I would request you," or "I would
entreat you, not to fear, not to tremble, my life for yours.

BOTTOM (Cont'd)

If you think I come hither as a lion, it were pity on my life.
No, I am no such thing. I am a man as other men are, and
there indeed let him name his name, and tell them, plainly, he
is Snuggles the Circus Midget.

QUINCE

Well it shall be so. But there are two hard things. That is, to
bring the moonlight into a chamber. For, you know, Pyramus
and Thisbe meet by moonlight.

SNOUT

Doth the moon shine that night we play our play?

BOTTOM

A calendar, a calendar! Look in the almanac, find out
moonshine, find out moonshine.

THEY run around to find a calendar.
SNUGGLES enters with a goofy calendar.
THEY crowd around to look at it.

QUINCE

Yes, it doth shine that night!

BOTTOM

Why, then may you leave a casement of the great chamber
window, where we play, open, and the moon may shine in at
the casement.

QUINCE

Ay, or else one must come in with a bush of thorns and a
lantern, and say he comes to disfigure, or to present, the
person of Moonshine. Then, there is another thing. We must
have a wall in the great chamber, for Pyramus and Thisbe
says the story, did talk through the chink of a wall.

SNOUT
You can never bring in a wall. What say you, Bottom?

BOTTOM
Some man or other must present Wall. Let him have some plaster, or some loam, or some rough-cast about him, to signify wall, and let him hold his fingers thus, and through that cranny shall Pyramus and Thisbe whisper.

QUINCE
If that may be, then all is well. Come, sit down, every mother's son, and rehearse your parts. Pyramus, you begin. When you have spoken your speech, enter into that brake, and so everyone according to his cue.

PUCK enters, unseen..

PUCK
What hempen home-spuns have we swaggering here? So near the cradle of the Fairy Queen? What, a play toward! I'll be an auditor, an actor too, perhaps, if I see cause.

QUINCE
Speak, Pyramus. Thisbe, stand forth.

BOTTOM
Thisbe, the flowers of odious savors sweet...

QUINCE
Odors, odors.

BOTTOM
...odors savors sweet. So hath thy breath, my dearest Thisbe dear. But hark, a voice! Stay thou but here awhile, and by and by, I will to thee appear.

BOTTOM exits.

PUCK

The weirdest Pyramus ever.

PUCK exits, following BOTTOM.

FLUTE

Must I speak now?

QUINCE

Ay, marry, must you, for you must understand he goes but to
see a noise that he heard, and is to come again.

FLUTE

Most radiant Pyramus, most lily-white of hue, of color like
the red rose on triumphant briar, most brisky juvenal and eke
most lovely Jew, as true as truest horse that yet would never
tire, I'll meet thee, Pyramus, at Ninny's tomb.

QUINCE

"Ninus' tomb", man. Why, you must not speak that yet, that
you answer to Pyramus. You speak all your part at once, cues
and all! Pyramus enter. Your cue is past, it is, "never tire."

FLUTE

Oh! ...as true as truest horse, that yet would never tire.

PUCK enters, and BOTTOM with a
donkey's head.

BOTTOM

If I were fair, Thisbe, I were only thine. HEE-HAW! HEE-
HAW!

QUINCE

O monstrous! O strange! We are haunted! Pray, masters! Fly,
masters! Help!

        RUDE MECHANICALS run about, tripping
        and stumbling all over the place. THEY
        finally exit, still screaming, leaving
        BOTTOM standing, bewildered.

BOTTOM

Was it something I said?

PUCK

I'll follow you, I'll lead you about a round, through bog,
through bush, through brake, through briar. Sometime a horse
I'll be, sometime a hound, a hog, a headless bear, sometime a
fire and neigh, and bark, and grunt, and roar, and burn, like
horse, hound, hog, bear, fire, at every turn.

        PUCK exits.

BOTTOM

Why do they run away? This is a knavery of them to make
me afeard.

        SNOUT enters.

SNOUT

Oh Bottom, thou art changed! What do I see on thee?

BOTTOM

What do you see?

        SNOUT exits. QUINCE enters.

QUINCE

Bless thee, Bottom! Bless thee! You've been bewitched.

        QUINCE exits.

BOTTOM

I see their knavery. This is to make fun of me, to frighten me,
if they could. But I will not stir from this place. I will walk
up and down and I will sing, that they shall hear I am not
afraid.
(HE sings.)
I've got a lovely bunch of coconuts. There they are a standing
in a row! Big ones, small ones, some as big as your head.
Give 'em a twist, a flick of the wrist, that's what the
showman said!

TITANIA
(Awaking)
What angel wakes me from my flowery bed?
(Sees him. SOUND: BOING!)
HUBBA-HUBBA-HUBBA!!!

BOTTOM

Say what?

TITANIA

I pray thee, gentle mortal, sing again. Mine ear is much
enamored of thy note. So is mine eye enthralled to thy shape
and thy fair virtue's force, perforce, doth move me. On the
first view to say, to swear, I love thee.

BOTTOM

Methinks, mistress, you should have little reason for that and
yet, to tell the truth, reason and love keep little company
together now-a-days. The more the pity that some honest
neighbors will not make them friends. Nay, I can gleek upon
occasion.

TITANIA

Thou art as wise as thou art beautiful.

BOTTOM

Not so, neither, but if I had wit enough to get out of this
wood, I have enough to serve mine own turn.

TITANIA

Out of this wood do not desire to go! Thou shalt remain here,
whether thou wilt or no. I am a spirit of no common rate. The
summer still doth tend upon my state, and I do love thee,
therefore, go with me. I'll give thee fairies to attend on thee,
and they shall fetch thee jewels from the deep, and sing while
thou on pressed flowers dost sleep. And I will purge thy
mortal grossness so that thou shalt like an airy spirit go.
Peaseblossom!

PEASEBLOSSOM

Ready.

TITANIA

Cobweb!

COBWEB

And I.

TITANIA

Moth!

MOTH

And I.

TITANIA

Mustardseed!

MUSTARDSEED

And I.

TITANIA

Little Indian Boy?

LITTLE INDIAN BOY
Sim, sim, sala bim.

ALL
Where shall we go?

TITANIA
Be kind and courteous to this gentleman. Dance at his side, in full view of his eyes. Feed him with apricots and blackberries. Bow to him, Fairies and do him courtesies.

PEASEBLOSSOM
Hail, mortal!

COBWEB
Hail!

MOTH
Hail!

MUSTARDSEED
Hail!

LITTLE INDIAN BOY
Sim, sim, sala bim!

BOTTOM
I cry your worship's mercy, heartily. I beseech your worship's name?

COBWEB
Cobweb.

BOTTOM
I shall desire you of more acquaintance, good Mistress Cobweb. If I cut my finger, I shall make bold with you. Your name, honest lady?

PEASEBLOSSOM

Peaseblossom.

BOTTOM

I pray you, commend me to Mistress Squash, your mother, and to Master Peascod, your father. Good Mistress Peaseblossom, I shall desire you of more acquaintance too. Your name, I beseech you, Madam?

MUSTARDSEED

Mustardseed.

BOTTOM

Good Mistress Mustardseed, I know your patience well. That same cowardly, giant-like ox-beef hath devoured many a gentleman of your house. I promise you, your kindred had made my eyes water ere now. I desire you of more acquaintance, good Mistress Mustardseed.

TITANIA

Come, wait upon him and lead him to my bower. The moon methinks looks with a watery eye and when she weeps, weeps every little flower, lamenting some enforced chastity.

BOTTOM

HEE-HAW!

TITANIA

(Aside to FAIRIES.)
Tie up my love's tongue. Bring him silently.

ALL exit. LIGHTS: BLACKOUT.

SCENE 6

OBERON enters.

OBERON
I wonder if Titania be awaked. Then, what it was that next came in her eye, which she must dote on in extremity.

PUCK enters, laughing.

OBERON
Here comes my messenger. How now, mad spirit?

PUCK
(Acting out what HE has seen.)
My mistress with a monster is in love! Near to her close and consecrated bower, while she was in her dull and sleeping hour, a crew of patches, rude mechanicals, that work for bread upon Athenian stalls were met together to rehearse a play intended for great Theseus' nuptial day. The shallowest thick skin of that barren sort, who Pyramus presented, forsook his scene and entered in a thicket. When I did him at this advantage take, a donkey's head I fixed on him. Anon his Thisbe must be answered and forth my mimic comes! When they him spy, as wild geese that the creeping fowler eye, sever themselves and madly sweep the sky, so at his sigh away his fellows fly! And at our stamp here over and over one falls, he "murder" cries and help from Athens calls! Their sense thus weak, lost with their fears thus strong, made senseless things begin to do them wrong. For briars and thorns at their apparel snatch, some sleeves, some hats, from yielders all things catch. I led them on in this distracted fear and left sweet Pyramus translated there. In that moment, so it came to pass, Titania waked and straightway loved an...aaa... a donkey!

OBERON

This falls out better than I could devise! But hast thou yet
latched the Athenian's eyes with the love-juice, as I did bid
thee do?

PUCK

I took him sleeping, that is finished too, and the Athenian
woman by his side, and when he waked, of force she must be
eyed.

HERMIA and DEMETRIUS enter.

OBERON

Stand close! This is the same Athenian.

PUCK

This is the woman, but not this the man.

DEMETRIUS

Oh, why rebuke you him that loves you so? Lay breath so
bitter on your bitter foe.

HERMIA

Now I but chide, but I should use thee worse, for thou, I fear,
hast given me cause to curse. If thou hast slain Lysander in
his sleep, being o'er shoes in blood, plunge in the deep, and
kill me too. It cannot be but thou hast murdered him. So
should a murderer look, so dead, so grim.

DEMETRIUS

So should the murdered look, and so should I, pierced
through the heart with your stern cruelty. Yet you, the
murderer, look as bright, as clear as yonder Venus in her
glimmering sphere.

HERMIA

What's this to my Lysander? Where is he? Ah, good
Demetrius, wilt thou give him me?

DEMETRIUS

I had rather give his carcass to my hounds.

HERMIA

Out, dog! Out, cur! Thou drivest me past the bounds of maiden's patience. Hast thou slain him, then? Henceforth be never numbered among men! Oh, once tell true, tell true, even for my sake! Durst thou have looked upon him being awake, and hast thou killed him sleeping? Oh brave touch! Could not a worm, an adder, do so much? An adder did it, for with doubler tongue than thine, thou serpent, never adder stung.

DEMETRIUS

You spend your passion on a misplaced mood. I am not guilty of Lysander's blood. Nor is he dead, for aught that I can tell.

HERMIA

I pray thee, tell me then that he is well.

DEMETRIUS

And if I could, what should I get therefore?

HERMIA

A privilege never to see me more. And from thy hated presence part I so. See me no more, whether he be dead or no.

SHE exits.

DEMETRIUS

There is no following her in this fierce vein. Here, therefore, for a while I will remain. So sorrow's heaviness doth heavier grow for debt that bankrupt sleep doth sorrow owe, which now in some slight measure it will pay, if for his tender here I make some stay.

HE lies down and sleeps.

OBERON
What hast thou done? Thou hast mistaken quite and laid the love-juice on some true-love's sight. Of thy misprision must perforce ensue some true love turned and not a false turned true.

PUCK
My bad!

OBERON
About the wood, go swifter than the wind, and Helena of Athens look thou find. All fancy-sick she is and pale of cheer, with sighs of love, that costs the fresh blood dear. By some illusion see thou bring her here. I'll charm his eyes against she do appear.

PUCK
I go, I go! Look how I go, swifter than arrow from the Tartar's bow.

MUSIC: WILLIAM TELL OVERTURE.
Someone throws HIM a stickhorse.

PUCK
HI-YO-SILVER-AWAY!

HE exits, riding.

OBERON
Flower of this purple dye, hit with Cupid's archery,
sink in apple of his eye. When his love he doth espy,
Let her shine as gloriously as the Venus of the sky.
When thou wakest, if she be by, beg of her for remedy.

PUCK enters, wearing army helmet.

PUCK
(Saluting.)

Captain of our fairy band, Helena is here at hand. And the youth, mistook by me, pleading for a lover's fee. Shall we their fond pageant see? Lord, what fools these mortals be!

OBERON

Stand aside. The noise they make will cause Demetrius to awake.

PUCK

Then will two at once woo one. That must needs be sport alone and those things do best please me that befall preposterously.

Enter LYSANDER and HELENA

LYSANDER

Why should you think that I should woo in scorn? Scorn and derision never come in tears. Look, when I vow, I weep, and vows so born, in their nativity all truth appears. How can these things in me seem scorn to you, bearing the badge of faith, to prove them true?

HELENA

You do advance your cunning more and more. When truth kills truth, O devilish-holy fray! These vows are Hermia's! Will you give her o'er? Weigh oath with oath, and you will nothing weigh. Your vows to her and me, put in two scales, will even weigh, and both as light as tales.

LYSANDER

I had no judgment when to her I swore.

HELENA

Nor none, in my mind, now you give her o'er.

LYSANDER
Demetrius loves her, and he loves not you!

DEMETRIUS
(Awaking. Spies HELENA. SOUND: BOING!)
HUBBA-HUBBA-HUBBA!!! Oh Helena, goddess, nymph, perfect, divine! To what, my love, shall I compare thine eye? Crystal is muddy. Oh, how ripe in show thy lips, those kissing cherries, tempting grow! That pure congealed white, high Taurus snow, fanned with the eastern wind, turns to a crow when thou hold'st up thy hand. Oh, let me kiss this princess of pure white, this seal of bliss!

HELENA
Oh spite! Oh cross! I see you all are bent to set against me for your merriment. If you were civil, and knew courtesy, you would not do me thus much injury. Can you not hate me as I know you do but you must join in souls to mock me too?

LYSANDER
You are unkind, Demetrius, be not so. For you love Hermia, this you know I know. Here, with all good will, with all my heart, in Hermia's love I yield you up my part and yours of Helena to me bequeath, whom I do love and will do till my death.

HELENA
Never did mockers waste more idle breath.

DEMETRIUS
Lysander, keep thy Hermia, I will none. If ever I loved her, all that love is gone. My heart to her but as guest-wise sojourned, and to Helena is it home returned, there to remain.

LYSANDER
Helena, it is not so.

DEMETRIUS

Disparage not the faith thou dost not know, lest, to thy peril, thou abide it dear. Look, where thy love comes. Yonder is thy dear.

Enter HERMIA.

HERMIA

Dark night, that from the eye his function takes, the ear more quick of apprehension makes, wherein it doth impair the seeing sense, it pays the hearing double recompense. Thou art not by mine eye, Lysander, found, mine ear, I thank it, brought me to thy sound. Dut why unkindly didst thou leave me so?

LYSANDER

Why should he stay, whom love doth press to go?

HERMIA

What love could press Lysander from my side?

LYSANDER

Lysander's love, that would not let him bide. Fair Helena, who more engilds the night than all you fiery odes and eyes of light. Why seekest thou me? Could not this make thee know, the hate I bear thee made me leave thee so?

HERMIA

You speak not as you think. It cannot be.

HELENA

Lo, she is one of this confederacy! Now I perceive they have conjoined all three to fashion this false sport, in spite of me. To join with men in scorning your poor friend? It is not friendly. Tis not maidenly. All women, as well as I, may chide you for it, though I alone do feel the injury.

HERMIA

I am amazed at your passionate words. I scorn you not. It
seems that you scorn me.

HELENA

Have you not set Lysander, as in scorn, to follow me and
praise my eyes and face? And made your other love,
Demetrius, who even but now did spurn me with his foot, to
call me goddess, nymph, divine and rare, precious, celestial?
Wherefore speaks he this to her he hates? And wherefore
doth Lysander deny your love, so rich within his soul, and
tender me, forsooth, affection, but by your setting on, by your
consent? What, though I be not so in grace as you, so hung
upon with love, so fortunate, but miserable most, to love
unloved? This you should pity rather than despise.

HERMIA

I know not what you mean by this.

HELENA

Ay, do, persevere, counterfeit sad looks, make faces at me
when I turn my back. Wink at each other and hold the sweet
jest up. This sport, well carried, shall be chronicled. If you
have any pity, grace, or manners, you would not make me
such an argument. But fare ye well. 'Tis partly my own fault,
which death or absence soon shall remedy.

LYSANDER

Stay, gentle Helena, hear my excuse. My love, my life, my
soul, fair Helena!

HELENA

Oh, excellent!

HERMIA

Sweet, do not scorn her so.

DEMETRIUS
If she cannot entreat, I can compel.

LYSANDER
Thou canst compel no more than she entreat. Thy threats
have no more strength than her weak prayers. Helena, I love
thee, by my life, I do. I swear by that which I will lose for
thee, to prove him false that says I love thee not.

DEMETRIUS
I say I love thee more than he can do.

LYSANDER
If thou say so, withdraw, and prove it too.

DEMETRIUS
Quick, come!

HERMIA
Lysander, whereto tends all this?

LYSANDER
Away, you leech!

DEMETRIUS
No, no, he'll seem to break loose, take on as you would
follow, but yet come not. You are a tame man, go!

LYSANDER
Hang off, thou cat, thou burr! Vile thing, let loose, or I will
shake thee from me like a serpent!

HERMIA
Why are you grown so rude? What change is this? Sweet
love...

LYSANDER

Thy love! Out, tawny Tartar, out! Out, loathed medicine!
Hated potion, hence!

HERMIA

Do you not jest?

HELENA

Yes, sooth, and so do you.

LYSANDER

Demetrius, I will keep my word with thee.

DEMETRIUS

I would I had your bond, for I perceive a weak bond holds
you. I'll not trust your word.

LYSANDER

What, should I hurt her, strike her, kill her dead? Although I
hate her, I'll not harm her so.

HERMIA

What, can you do me greater harm than hate? Hate me!
Wherefore? Oh, me! What news, my love! Am not I Hermia?
Are not you Lysander? I am as fair now as I was erewhile.
Since night you loved me, yet since night you left me. Why,
then you left me, the gods forbid, in earnest, shall I say?

LYSANDER

Ay, by my life and never did desire to see thee more.
Therefore be out of hope, of question, of doubt. Be certain,
nothing truer, 'tis no jest that I do hate thee and love Helena.

HERMIA

You juggler! You canker-blossom! You thief of love! What,
have you come by night and stolen my love's heart from him?

HELENA

That's rich! Have you no modesty, no maiden shame, no touch of bashfulness? What, will you tear impatient answers from my gentle tongue? Fie, fie! You counterfeit, you puppet, you!

HERMIA

Puppet? Why so? Oh, that way goes the game. Now I perceive that she hath made compare between our statures. She hath urged her height, and with her personage, her tall personage, her height, forsooth, she hath prevailed with him. And are you grown so high in his esteem because I am so dwarfish and so low? How low am I, thou painted maypole? Speak! How low am I? I am not yet so low but that my nails can reach unto thine eyes!

HELENA

I pray you, though you mock me, gentlemen, let her not hurt me. I was never curst, I have no gift at all in shrewishness. I am a right maid for my cowardice. Let her not strike me. You perhaps may think, because she is something lower than myself, that I can match her.

HERMIA

Lower! Hark, again!

HELENA

Good Hermia, do not be so bitter with me. I evermore did love you.

HERMIA

Get you gone! What is it that hinders you?

HELENA

A foolish heart, that I leave here behind!

HERMIA

What, with Lysander?

HELENA

With Demetrius!

LYSANDER

Be not afraid, she shall not harm thee, Helena.

DEMETRIUS

No, sir, she shall not, though you take her part.

HELENA

Oh, when she's angry, she is keen and shrewd. She was a vixen when she went to school, and though she be but little, she is fierce.

HERMIA

Little again? Nothing but low and little? Why will you suffer her to flout me thus? Let me come to her!

LYSANDER

Get you gone, you dwarf! You minimus of hindering knot-grass made! You bead! You acorn!

OBERON and PUCK

Oh snap!

DEMETRIUS

You are too officious in her behalf that scorns your services.

LYSANDER

Now she holds me not. Let's take this outside!

DEMETRIUS

We are outside.

LYSANDER
(Looking around.)
Touché. Then let's take this...over there!

DEMETRIUS

Over there, it is!

THEY exit.

HERMIA

This is all your fault!

HELENA starts to leave.

HERMIA

No! Don't go!

HELENA

I will not trust you. I will no longer stay in your company.
Your hands than mine are quicker for a fray, but my legs are
longer, though to run away.

SHE exits.

HERMIA

I am amazed, and know not what to say.

SHE exits, OBERON and PUCK come out
from behind the tree.

OBERON

This is thy negligence. Mistakes again, or else you're up to
your roguish tricks on purpose!

PUCK

Believe me, Sir. I mistook. But you gotta admit, it's pretty
funny!

OBERON

No.

PUCK

Kinda funny?

OBERON

No.

PUCK

Mildly amusing?

OBERON

Ehhhh. You can see that these lovers are looking for a place
to go fight. Therefore, Puck, you must go and cloud the night.
Cover the forest with a thick fog. Keep them apart until
morning. Use this flower to release them from their spell.
(Hands PUCK a flower.)
While you are doing this, I will go to my Queen. I'll set her
free from the spell that binds her to the monster and all will
be at peace!

PUCK

My fair lord, this must be done quickly. Night is swiftly
passing from the sky.

OBERON

Then what are you waiting for?

PUCK

What else? Chase music! Hit it!

Chase music begins. THEY exit. PUCK
enters with fog machine. A long and comical
chase scene ensues with the end result that
the FOUR LOVERS are fast asleep side by
side. LIGHTS: FADE OUT.

INTERMISSION. (If desired.)

SCENE 7

LIGHTS: RISE as TITANIA, BOTTOM
and FAIRIES enter. OBERON enters and
hides behind a tree.

TITANIA
Come sit with me, handsome!

BOTTOM
Where's Peaseblossom?

PEASEBLOSSOM
Ready!

BOTTOM
Scratch my head, Peaseblossom. Where's Cobweb?

COBWEB
Ready!

BOTTOM
Mistress Cobweb. Get your weapons ready and go kill me a
red hipped bumblebee on the top of a thistle. And bring me
some honeycomb, Madam. But do be careful Mistress
Cobweb. Honeycomb's big yeah, yeah, yeah, it's not small,
no, no, no. Where's Mistress Mustardseed?

MUSTARDSEED
Ready!

BOTTOM
Give me your hand, Mistress Mustardseed.

THEY shake hands.

MUSTARDSEED
What's shaking?

BOTTOM

Nothing. I thought you might help Mistress Peaseblossom scratch my head.
(Feels HIS chin.)
I must to the barber's, Sir, for methinks I am marvelous hairy about the face.

TITANIA

Are you hungry, my love?

BOTTOM

Truly. How about some fodder? I could munch on some good dry oats. Methinks, I have a great desire for a bundle of hay. Good hay. Sweet hay. Mmmmmm...hay! But right now I would rather not be bothered. I have an exposition of sleep come upon me.

TITANIA

Sleep then, my love. I will send my Fairies to fetch it for you. Fairies, be gone, and be all ways away.

> FAIRIES exit. BOTTOM and TITANIA fall asleep. OBERON crosses to THEM.

OBERON

(Touching flower to TITANIA'S eyelids.)
Be as thou have always been.
See as thou have always seen.
Diana's bud over Cupid's flower,
Hath such force and blessed power.

Now my Titania, wake you, my sweet Queen.

> TITANIA awakes, looks around.

TITANIA

My Oberon! What visions have I seen! Methought I was enamored of an...aaa...a donkey.

OBERON

There lies your love.

HE points to BOTTOM.

TITANIA

Say what? How can these things come to pass? Oh, how mine eyes loathe his visage now!

OBERON

Silence awhile. Puck, take off this head.

PUCK
(Removing the donkey head.)
Now, when thou wakes with thine own fool's eyes peep.

OBERON

Come, my Queen, take hands with me, and rock the ground whereon these sleepers be. Now, thou and I are new in amity, and will tomorrow midnight solemnly dance in Duke Theseus' house triumphantly. And bless it to all fair prosperity. There shall the pairs of faithful lovers be wedded, with Theseus, all in jollity.

PUCK

Fairy King, attend and mark, I do hear the morning lark.
(Crows like a rooster.)

OBERON

Then, my Queen, in silence sad, trip we after night's shade. We, the globe can compass soon, swifter than the wandering moon.

TITANIA

Come, my lord and in our flight, tell me how it came this night that I sleeping here was found, with these mortals on the ground.

OBERON
Well, you see, it's a funny story...

LIGHTS: BLACKOUT.

SCENE 8

LIGHTS: RISE on the LOVERS asleep on the ground.
        AEGEUS, THESEUS and HIPPOLYTA enter.

HIPPOLYTA

What is this?

EGEUS

My lord, this is my daughter here asleep. And this is
Lysander. This Demetrius is. This Helena, old Nedar's
Helena. I wonder about their being here together.

THESEUS

No doubt they rose early to observe the rite of May, and
hearing of our intentions, came here to honor our ceremonies.
But tell me, Egeus, isn't this the day that Hermia should
announce her intentions?

EGEUS

It is, my lord.

THESEUS

Wake them.

EGEUS pokes them with a stick.

THESEUS

Good morrow, friends. Saint Valentine is past.

THEY awake and stand up in a panic.

LYSANDER

Pardon, my lord!

THEY kneel.

THESEUS

I pray you all, stand up. I know you two are rival enemies.
How comes this gentle concord in the world, that hatred is so
far from jealousy to sleep by hate, and fear no hostility?

LYSANDER

My lord. I shall reply, amazedly. Half asleep, half waking.
But as yet I swear, I cannot truly say how I came here. But as
I think, for truly would I speak, as now I do bethink me, so it
is...I came with Hermia hither. Our intent was to be gone
from Athens, where we might without the peril of Athenian
law...

EGEUS

Enough! Enough, my lord! You have enough! I beg the law!
The law upon his head. They would have stolen away,
Demetrius. Thereby to have defeated you and me. You of
your wife, and me, of my consent, that she should be your
wife.

DEMETRIUS

My lord. Fair Helena told me of their secret flight and their
reasons for coming to this wood. I followed them here in
anger, and fair Helena followed me out of deepest love...for
me. But, my lord, I don't know by what power, but by some
power...my love for Hermia melted like the snow. My whole
life, my whole heart now belongs to Helena.

HIPPOLYTA whispers in THESEUS' ear.

THESEUS

Fair lovers, you are fortunately met. Of this discourse we will
hear anon. Egeus, I will overbear your will. For in the temple
by and by with us these couples shall eternally be knit. Away
with us to Athens, three and three, and we'll hold a feast.
Come, Hippolyta.

THEY exit.

BOTTOM
(Awaking.)
When my cue comes, call me, and I will answer.
(Looks around.)
Hello? Anybody? Hello? Peter Quince? Flute? Stout?
Starveling? Stolen hence, and left asleep! I have had a most
rare vision. I've had a dream beyond a man's ability to say
what the dream was. Any man trying to interpret it would
make a...donkey of himself. Me thought, I was a...Me thought
I had a.... A man would be a patched fool if he were to say
what me thought I had. The eye of man has not heard, the ear
of man hath not seen, man's hand is not able to taste, his
tongue to conceive, nor his heart to report, what my dream
was. I will get Peter Quince to write a ballad of this dream,
and it should be called "Bottom's Dream", because it hath no
bottom. I will sing it in the latter end of the play, before the
Duke. To make it more pleasing, I will sing it at Thisbe's
death.

HE exits running. LIGHTS: FADE OUT.

SCENE 9

QUINCE, FLUTE, SNOUT, and STARVELING
enter.

QUINCE.
Have you sent to Bottom's house? Is he come home yet?

STARVELING
He cannot be heard of. No doubt, he is transported!

FLUTE
If he come not, then the play is marred. It goes not forward,
doth it?

QUINCE
It is not possible. You have not a man in all Athens able to
discharge Pyramus, but he.

FLUTE
No, he hath simply the best wit of any handicraft man in
Athens.

QUINCE
Yea and the best person too, and he is a very paramour for a
sweet voice.

FLUTE
You must say "paragon". A paramour is, God bless us, a
naughty person.

SNUGGLES enters.

SNUGGLES
Masters, the Duke is coming from the temple, and there is
two or three lords and ladies more married. If we could have
done our play, we would have been rich. Cha-ching!

FLUTE

Oh, sweet, bully Bottom! Thus hath he lost sixpence a day
during his life. He could not have escaped sixpence a day.
Had the Duke not given him sixpence a day for playing
Pyramus, I'll be hanged. He would have deserved it. Sixpence
a day in Pyramus, or nothing.

BOTTOM enters.

BOTTOM

Where are these lads? Where are these hearts?

QUINCE

Bottom! Oh, most courageous day! Oh, most happy hour!

BOTTOM

Masters, I am to discourse wonders. But ask me not what, for
if I tell you, I am no true Athenian. I will tell you everything,
right as it fell out.

QUINCE

Let us hear, sweet Bottom.

BOTTOM

Not a word of me. All that I will tell you is that the Duke
hath dined!

(THEY cover THEIR eyes.)

Get your costumes together!

(THEY cover THEIR ears.)

Go over your parts!

(THEY cover THEIR mouths.)

Our play has been chosen! Oh, yes. Don't eat any onions or
garlic for we must have sweet smelling breath, then they will
say it is a sweet smelling comedy! To the palace!

THEY exit.

LIGHTS: BLACKOUT

SCENE 10

THESEUS, HIPPOLYTA, EGEUS,
HERMIA, LYSANDER, HELENA,
DEMETRIUS and PHILOSTRATE enter.

THESEUS
Philostrate, say what entertainment we have for this evening?
What play? What music? How shall we celebrate this
occasion?

PHILOSTRATE
Here is a list of all the shows that are ready, Sir. Choose
which one you like.

Hands THESEUS a program.

THESEUS
(Reading.)
The Battle of the Centaurs, to be sung by an Athenian
eunuch, to the harp.

DEMETRIUS
What's a eunuch?

CAST
Nevermind.

THESEUS
"So, Who Was That Masked Guy Anyway? A comedy in
which the poop hits the fans." I saw that one already. I didn't
like it. Say...what is this one? A tedious, brief scene of young
Pyramus and his love Thisbe. Very tragical mirth. Merry and
tragical? Tedious and brief? That is hot ice and wondrous
strange snow. How shall we follow this nonsense?

PHILOSTRATE

A play there is my Lord, some ten words long, which is as
brief as I have known a play. But by ten words, my Lord, it is
too long, which makes it tedious, for in all the play there is
not one word apt or one player fitted. And tragical, my noble
Lord, it is, for Pyramus therin doth kill himself, which I saw
rehearsed and I must confess, made mine eyes water, but
more merry tears, the passion of laughter never shed.

HIPPOLYTA

Who is it that puts this play on?

PHILOSTRATE

Common laborers, who never did anything intellectual
before, but who have forced their rusty brains to memorize
this play to celebrate your wedding.

THESEUS

Then we will hear it.

PHILOSTRATE

No, my noble Lord. It is not for you. I have heard it
over...and...it stinks.

THESEUS

I will hear that play, for never can anything be amiss when
simpleness and duty tender it. Go, bring them in, and we
shall take our places.

PHILOSTRATE exits.

HIPPOLYTA

I love not to see wretchedness overcharged, and duty in his
service perishing.

THESEUS

Why, gentle sweet, you shall see no such thing.

HIPPOLYTA
But dear, he said they stink.

THESEUS
Shhh. It's starting.

PHILOSTRATE enters.

PHILOSTRATE
So please your grace, the Prologue is addressed.

QUINCE enters.

QUINCE
(Nervous, speaking too quickly.)
If we offend, it is with our good will that you should think,
we come not to offend, but with good will. To show our
simple skill, that is the true beginning of our end. Consider
then we come but in despite. We do not come as minding to
contest you, our true intent is all for your delight. We are not
here that you should here repent you. The actors are at hand
and by their show, you shall know all that you are like to
know.
(Sighs in relief that HE got through it.)

THESEUS
This fellow doth not stand upon points.

LYSANDER
He hath rid his Prologue like a rough colt. He knows not
when to stop. A good moral, my Lord, it is not enough to
speak, but to speak true.

HIPPOLYTA
Indeed he hath played on his Prologue like a child on a
recorder. A sound, but not in tune.

THESEUS

His speech was like a tangled chain, nothing impaired, but all disordered. Who is next?

PYRAMUS, THISBE, WALL,
MOONSHINE, and LION enter.

QUINCE

Gentles, perchance you wonder at this show. But wonder on, till truth make all things plain. This man is Pyramus, if you would know. This beauteous lady Thisbe is certain. This man, with lime and rough-cast, doth present Wall, that vile Wall which did these lovers sunder. And through Wall's chink, poor souls, they are content to whisper, at which let no man wonder. This man, with lantern, dog, and bush of thorn, presenteth Moonshine, for, if you will know, by moonshine did these lovers think no scorn to meet at Ninus' tomb, there to woo. This grisly beast, which Lion hight by name, the trusty Thisbe, coming first by night, did scare away, or rather did affright. As she fled, her mantle she did fall, which Lion vile with bloody mouth did stain. Anon comes Pyramus, sweet youth and tall, and finds his trusty Thisbe's mantle slain. Whereat, with blade, with bloody blameful blade, he bravely broached is boiling bloody breast and Thisbe, tarrying in mulberry shade, his dagger drew, and died. For all the rest, let Lion, Moonshine, Wall, and lovers twain at large discourse, while here they do remain.

THISBE, LION and MOONSHINE exit.

THESEUS

I wonder if the lion be to speak.

DEMETRIUS

No wonder, my lord. One lion may, when many donkeys do.

WALL

In this same interlude, it doth befall that I, one Snout by name, present a wall. Such a wall, as I would have you think, that had in it a crannied hole or chink. Through which the lovers, Pyramus and Thisbe, did whisper often, very secretly. This loam, this rough-cast and this stone doth show that I am that same wall, the truth is so. And this the cranny is, right and sinister, through which the fearful lovers are to whisper.

THESEUS

Would you desire lime and hair to speak better?

DEMETRIUS

It is the wittiest partition that ever I heard discourse, my lord.

PYRAMUS enters.

THESEUS

Pyramus draws near the wall, silence!

PYRAMUS

Oh, grim-looked night! Oh, night with hue so black! Oh, night, which ever art when day is not! Oh, night! Oh, night! alack, alack, alack, I fear my Thisbe's promise is forgot! And thou, oh, wall, oh, sweet, oh, lovely wall, that stand'st between her father's ground and mine! Thou wall, oh, wall, oh, sweet and lovely wall, show me thy chink, to blink through with mine eye!

WALL holds up HIS fingers.

PYRAMUS

Thanks, courteous wall, Jove shield thee well for this! But what see I? No Thisbe do I see. Oh, wicked wall, through whom I see no bliss! Cursed be thy stones for thus deceiving me!

THESEUS
The wall, methinks, being sensible, should curse again.

PYRAMUS
No, in truth, sir, he should not. "Deceiving me" is Thisbe's cue. She is to enter now, and I am to spy her through the wall. You shall see, it will fall pat as I told you. Yonder she comes.

THISBE enters.

THISBE
Oh, wall, full often hast thou heard my moans, for parting my fair Pyramus and me! My cherry lips have often kissed thy stones, thy stones with lime and hair knit up in thee.

PYRAMUS
I see a voice! Now will I to the chink, to spy and I can hear my Thisbe's face. Thisbe!

THISBE
My love thou art, my love I think.

PYRAMUS
Think what thou wilt, I am thy lover's grace and, like Limander, am I trusty still.

THISBE
And I like Helen, till the Fates me kill.

PYRAMUS
Not Shafalus to Procrus was so true.

THISBE
As Shafalus to Procrus, I to you.

PYRAMUS
Oh, kiss me through the hole of this vile wall!

THISBE
I kiss the wall's hole, not your lips at all.

PYRAMUS
Wilt thou at Ninny's tomb meet me straight away?

QUINCE
Ninus' tomb!

PYRAMUS
Wilt thou at <u>Ninus'</u> tomb meet me straight away?

THISBE
'Tide life, 'tide death, I come without delay.

PYRAMUS and THISBE exit.

WALL
Thus have I, Wall, my part discharged so and, being done, thus Wall away doth go.

WALL exits.

THESEUS
Now is the mural down between the two neighbors.

DEMETRIUS
No remedy, my lord, when walls are so willful to hear without warning.

HIPPOLYTA
This is the silliest stuff that ever I heard.

THESEUS
The best in this kind are but shadows and the worst are no worse, if imagination amends them.

HIPPOLYTA
It must be your imagination then, and not theirs.

THESEUS
If we imagine no worse of them than they of themselves, they may pass for excellent men. Here come two noble beasts in, a man and a lion.

MOONSHINE and LION enter.

LION
You, ladies, you, whose gentle hearts do fear the smallest monstrous mouse that creeps on floor, may now perchance both quake and tremble here, when lion rough in wildest rage doth roar. Roawr! Roawr! Then know that I, one Snuggles am, a lion-fell, nor else no lion's dam, for, if I should as lion come in strife into this place, 'twere pity on my life.

THESEUS
A very gentle beast and of a good conscience.

DEMETRIUS
The very best at a beast, my Lord, that ever I saw.

LYSANDER
This lion is a very fox for his valor.

THESEUS
True, and a goose for his discretion.

DEMETRIUS
Not so, my Lord, for his valor cannot carry his discretion and the fox carries the goose.

THESEUS
His discretion, I am sure, cannot carry his valor for the goose carries not the fox. It is well. Leave it to his discretion, and let us listen to the moon.

MOONSHINE

This lantern doth the horned moon present...

DEMETRIUS

He should have worn the horns on his head.

THESEUS

He is no crescent, and his horns are invisible within the circumference.

MOONSHINE

This lantern doth the horned moon present, myself the man in the moon do seem to be.

THESEUS

This is the greatest error of all the rest. The man should be put into the lantern. How is it else the man in the moon?

DEMETRIUS

He dares not come there for the candle, for, you see, it is already in snuff.

HIPPOLYTA

I am aweary of this moon! Would he would change!

THESEUS

It appears, by his small light of discretion, that he is in the wane. But yet, in courtesy, in all reason, we must stay the time.

LYSANDER

Proceed, Moon.

MOONSHINE

All that I have to say, is, to tell you that the lantern is the moon. I, the man in the moon, this thorn-bush, my thorn-bush and this dog, my dog.

DEMETRIUS
Why, all these should be in the lantern, for all these are in the moon. But, silence! Here comes Thisbe.

THISBE enters.

THISBE
This is old Ninny's tomb. Where is my love?

WHOLE CAST
NINUS' TOMB!

LION
RAWWWRRRRR!!!!

THISBE runs off, screaming. Falls down, gets up, exits.

DEMETRIUS
Well roared, Lion.

THESEUS
Well run, Thisbe.

HIPPOLYTA
Well shone, Moon. Truly, the moon shines with a good grace.

THE LION shakes THISBE'S mantle, and exits.

THESEUS
Well moused, Lion.

LYSANDER
And so the lion vanished.

DEMETRIUS

And then came Pyramus.

PYRAMUS enters.

PYRAMUS

Sweet Moon, I thank thee for thy sunny beams. I thank thee, Moon, for shining now so bright, for, by thy gracious, golden, glittering gleams, I trust to take of truest Thisbe's sight. But stay, oh, spite! But mark, poor knight, what dreadful dole is here! Eyes, do you see? How can it be? Oh, dainty duck! Oh, dear! Thy mantle good, what, stained with blood! Approach, ye Furies fell! Oh, Fates, come, come, cut thread and thrum, quail, crush, conclude, and quell!

THESEUS

This passion, and the death of a dear friend, would go near to make a man look sad.

HIPPOLYTA

Beshrew my heart, but I pity the man.

PYRAMUS

Oh, wherefore, Nature, didst thou lions frame? Since lion vile hath here devoured my dear, which is...no, no...which <u>was</u> the fairest dame that lived, that loved, that liked, that looked with cheer. Come, tears, confound, out sword, and wound the pap of Pyramus.

> (Stabs HIMSELF in right side. Realizes it's the
> wrong side. Stabs HIMSELF in left side.)

Ay, that left pap, where heart doth hop. Thus die I, thus, thus, thus. Now, am I dead. Now, am I fled. My soul is in the sky. Tongue, lose thy light and moon, take thy flight. Now die, die, die, die, die.

HE dies.

DEMETRIUS

No die, but an ace, for him, for he is but one.

LYSANDER

Less than an ace, man, for he is dead. He is nothing.

THESEUS

With the help of a surgeon he might yet recover.

HIPPOLYTA

How chance Moonshine is gone before Thisbe comes back
and finds her lover?

THESEUS

She will find him by starlight. Here she comes and her
passion ends the play.

THISBE enters.

HIPPOLYTA

Methinks she should not use a long one for such a Pyramus. I
hope she will be brief.

DEMETRIUS

A mote will turn the balance, which Pyramus, which Thisbe,
is the better. He for a man, God warrant us. She for a woman,
God bless us.

LYSANDER

She hath spied him already with those sweet eyes.

DEMETRIUS

And thus she moans, thusly...

THISBE

Asleep, my love? What, dead, my dove? Oh, Pyramus, arise!
Speak, speak. Quite dumb? Dead, dead? A tomb must cover
thy sweet eyes. These, my lips, this cherry nose, these yellow
cowslip cheeks, are gone, are gone. Lovers, make moan. His
eyes were green as leeks. Oh, Sisters Three, come, come to
me, with hands as pale as milk. Lay them in gore, since you
have shore with shears his thread of silk. Tongue, not a word.
Come, trusty sword, come, blade, my breast imbrue.
(Stabs HERSELF.)
And, farewell, friends, thus Thisbe ends. Adieu, adieu, adieu.

SHE dies.

THESEUS

Moonshine and Lion are left to bury the dead.

DEMETRIUS

Ay, and Wall too.

BOTTOM
(Sits up.)
No, I assure you, the wall is down that parted their fathers.
Will it please you to see the Epilogue, or to hear a
Bergomask dance between two of our company?

THESEUS

No Epilogue, I pray you, for your play needs no excuse.
Never excuse, for when the players are all dead, there needs
none to be blamed. Marry, if he that writ it had played
Pyramus and hanged himself in Thisbe's garter, it would have
been a fine tragedy. And so it is, truly, and very notably
discharged. And now the iron tongue of midnight hath tolled
twelve. Lovers, to bed. 'Tis almost fairy time.

THEY exit. PUCK enters.

PUCK

If we shadows have offended,
think but this, and all is mended,
that you have but slumbered here,
whqile these visions did appear.
And this weak and idle theme,
no more yielding but a dream.
Gentles, do not reprehend,
if you pardon, we will mend.
And, as I am an honest Puck,
if we have unearned luck.
Now to escape the serpent's tongue,
we will make amends ere long.
Else the Puck a liar call,
so, good night unto you all.
Give me your hands, if we be friends,
and Robin shall restore amends.

HE exits. LIGHTS: FADE TO BLACK.

THE END

Thank you for purchasing and reading this play. If you enjoyed it, we'd appreciate a review on Amazon.com.

On the following pages you will find a selection of other plays from the Black Box Theatre Publishing Company catalog presented for you at no additional cost.

Enjoy!!!

www.blackboxtheatrepublishing.com

NOW AVAILABLE!!!

"Poop Happens!" in this family friendly cowboy comedy!

So, Who Was That Masked Guy Anyway? is the story of Ernie, the grandson of the original Masked Cowboy, a lawman who fought for truth, justice and the cowboy way in the old west. Now that Grandpa is getting on in years he's looking for someone to carry on for him. The only problem? Ernie doesn't know anything about being a cowboy. He's never seen a real cow, he's allergic to milk and to tell the truth he doesn't know one end of a horse from another...but beware, before it's all over, the poop is sure to hit the fans!

Cast Size: 21 Flexible M-F Roles Doubling Possible.

Royalties: $50.00 per performance.

Running Time: Approximately 90 minutes.

NOW AVAILABLE!!!

WANTED: SANTA CLAUS is the story of what happens when a group of department store moguls decide to replace Santa Claus with the shiny new "KRINGLE 3000", codenamed...ROBO-SANTA! Now it's up to Santa's elves to save the day! But Santa's in no shape to take on his stainless steel counterpart! He'll have to train for his big comeback. Enter Mickey, one of the toughest elves of all time! He'll get Santa ready for the big showdown! But it's going to mean reaching deep down inside to find "the eye of the reindeer"!

Cast Size 23 Flexible M-F Roles Doubling Possible.

Royalties: $50.00 per performance.

Running Time: Approximately 90 Minutes.

NOW AVAILABLE!!!

At the edge of the universe sits The Long John Cafe. A place where the average guy and the average "Super" guy can sit and have a cup of coffee and just be themselves...or, someone else if that's what they want. The cafe is populated by iconic figures of the 20th Century, including cowboys, hippies, super heroes and movie stars. They've come to celebrate the end of the old Century and the beginning of tomorrow! That is, if they make it through the night! It seems the evil Dr. McNastiman has other plans for our heroes. Like their total destruction!

Cast Size: 17 9M 8F.

Royalties: $50.00 per performance.

Running Time: Approximately 90 Minutes.

NOW AVAILABLE!!!

Jacklyn Sparrow and the Lady Pirates of the Caribbean is our brand new swashbuckling pirate parody complete with bloodthirsty buccaneers in massive sword clanking battle scenes!! A giant wise cracking parrot named Polly!! Crazy obsessions with eye liner!! And just who is Robert, the Dreaded Phylum Porifera!!!

Please Note: We offer large and small cast versions of this play. Cast and royalty numbers for both are below.

Cast Size: 45/13 Flexible M-F Roles Doubling Possible.

Royalties: $50.00 per performance.

Running Time: Approximately120/45 Minutes.

NOW AVAILABLE!!!

"May the Dwarf be with you in this wacky take on the classic fairy tale which will have audiences rolling in the floor with laughter!

What happens when you mix an articulate mirror, a conceited queen, a prince dressed in purple, seven little people with personality issues, a basket of kumquats and a little Star Wars for good measure?

Cast Size: 12 Flexible M-F Roles.

Royalty: $50.00 per performance.

Running Time: Approximately 45 Minutes.

NOW AVAILABLE!!!

"My dreams of thee flow softly.
They enter with tender rush.
The still soft sound which echoes,
When I lower the lid and flush."

They say that porcelain is the best antenna for creativity. At least that's what this cast of young people believe in Dear John: An ode to the potty! The action of this one act play takes place almost entirely behind the doors of five bathroom stalls. This short comedy is dedicated to all those term papers, funny pages and Charles Dickens' novels that have been read behind closed (stall) doors!

Cast Size: 10 5M 5F.

Royalties: $35.00 per performance.

Running Time: Approximately 15 Minutes.

NOW AVAILABLE!!!

Declassified after 40 years!

On December 21, 1970, an impromptu meeting took place between the King of Rock and Roll and the Leader of the Free World.

Elvis Meets Nixon (Operation Wiggle) is a short comedy which offers one possible (and ultimately ridiculous) explanation of what happened during that meeting.

Cast Size: 2 M with 1 Offstage F Voice.

Royalties: $35.00 per performance.

Running Time: Approximately 10 Minutes.

NOW AVAILABLE!!!

In the beginning, there was a man.
Then there was a woman.
And then there was this piece of fruit...
...and that's when everything went horribly wrong!
Even Adam is a short comedy exploring the relationship
between men and women right from day one.

Why doesn't he ever bring her flowers like he used to?
Why doesn't she laugh at his jokes anymore?
And just who is that guy in the red suit?
And how did she convince him to eat that fruit, anyway?

Cast Size: 3 2M-1F.

Royalties: $35.00 per performance.

Running Time: Approximately 10 Minutes.

NOW AVAILABLE!!!

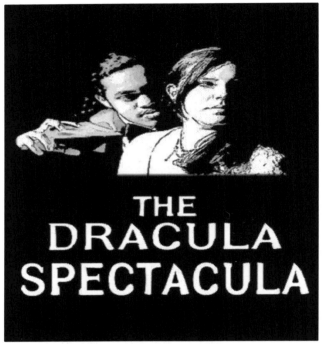

Count Dracula is bored. He's pretty much sucked
Transylvania dry, and he's looking for a new challenge. So
it's off to New York, New York! The Big Apple! The town
that never sleeps...that'll pose a challenge for sure.
Dracula purchases The Carfax Theatre and decides to put on
a big, flashy Broadway show!

Cast Size: 50 Flexible M/F roles with Doubling Possible.

Royalties: $50.00 per performance.

Running Time: Approximately 90 Minutes.

NOW AVAILABLE!!!

THE FOUR PRESIDENTS is an educational play which examines the lives and characters of four of the most colorful personalities to hold the office. George Washington, Abraham Lincoln, Theodore Roosevelt and Richard Nixon. Much of the dialogue comes from the Presidents' own words.

A perfect show for schools!

Cast Size: 10 Flexible M-F Roles with Doubling Possible.

Royalties: $50.00 per performance.

Running Time: Approximately 60 Minutes.

NOW AVAILABLE!!!

The lights rise on a beautiful sunset.
A mermaid is silhouetted against an ocean backdrop.
Hauntingly familiar music fills the air.
Then...the Lawyer shows up.
And that's when the fun really begins!

It's The Little Mermaid (More or Less.)

Cast Size: 30 Flexible M-F Roles with Doubling Possible.

Royalties: $50.00 per performance.

Running Time: Approximately 45 Minutes.

NOW AVAILABLE!!!

Cinderella and the Quest for the Crystal Pump, is the story of a young girl seeking a life beyond the endless chores heaped upon her by her grouchy stepmother and two stepsisters. But more than anything, Cinderella wants to go to the prince's masquerade ball, but there's one problem...she has nothing to wear! Luckily, her Fairy Godperson has a few ideas.

Please Note: This play is available in large and small cast versions. Both cast sizes and royalty rates are listed below.

Cast Size: 30/13 Flexible M-F Roles with Some Doubling Possible.

Royalties: $50.00 per performance.

Running Time: Approximately 90/45 Minutes.

NOW AVAILABLE!!!

Shorespeare is loosely based on a Midsummer Night's Dream.
Shakespeare, with the help of Cupid, has landed at the Jersey Shore.
Cupid inspires him to write a play about two New Jersey
sweethearts, Cleo and Toni. Shakespeare is put off by their accent
and way of talking, but decides to send the two teenagers on a
course of true love. Toni and Cleo are determined to get married
right after they graduate from high school, but in order to do so they
must pass this course of true love that Cupid's pixies create and
manipulate. As they travel along the boardwalk at the Jersey Shore,
Cleo and Toni, meet a handful of historical figures disguised as the
carnies. Confucius teaches Cleo the "Zen of Snoring", Charles
Ponzi teaches them the importance of "White Lies", Leonardo Da
Vinci shows them the "Art of Multitasking", and finally they meet
Napolean who tries to help them to "Accept Shortcomings" of each
other. After going through all these lessons, the sweethearts decide
that marriage should wait, and Cupid is proud of Shakespeare who
has finally reached out to the modern youth.

NOW AVAILABLE!!!

Everyone has heard the phrase, "it's the squeaky wheel that gets the oil," but how many people know the Back-story? The story begins in a kingdom far, far away over the rainbow – a kingdom called Spokend. This kingdom of wheels is a happy one for the gods have blessed the tiny hamlet with plentiful sunshine, water and most important –oil. Until a terrible drought starts to dry up all the oil supplies. What is to be done?

The powerful barons of industry and politicians decide to hold a meeting to decide how to solve the situation. Since Spokend is a democracy all the citizens come to the meeting but their voices are ignored – especially the voice of one of the poorer citizens of the community suffering from a squeak that can only be cured with oil, Spare Wheel and his wife Fifth Wheel. Despite Spare Wheel's desperate pleas for oil, he is ignored and sent home without any help or consideration.

Without oil, Spare Wheel's squeak becomes so bad he loses his job and his family starts to suffer when his sick leave and unemployment benefits run out. What is he to do? Spare Wheel and Fifth Wheel develop a scheme that uses the squeak to their advantage against the town magistrate Big Wheel who finally relents and gives over the oil. Thus, for years after in the town of Spokend citizens in need of help are told "It's the squeaky wheel that gets the oil."

NOW AVAILABLE!!!

Once upon a time, a beautiful princess was placed under a magic spell by an evil fairy. A spell that would cause her to fall into a deep, deep sleep. A sleep from which she would awaken 1000 years later.
It's "Sleeping Beauty meets Buck Rogers" in this play for young audiences.

Royalties: $50.00 per performance.

Cast Size: 13 with flexible extras.

Running Time: Approximately 45 minutes.

NOW AVAILABLE!!!

Santa Claus. Frosty. Rudolph. Jack Frost.

This Christmas…if you've got a problem and if you can find them then maybe you can hire…THE SLEIGH TEAM!!!

The team is hired by lowly clerk, Bob Crachit to help his boss, the miserly old Ebenezer Scrooge find a little "Christmas Spirit"!

Royalties: $50.00 per performance.

Cast Size: 6

Running Time: Approximately 45 minutes.

NOW AVAILABLE!!!

The Odd Princesses is a parody/mash-up that opens with a group of princesses assembled for a card game in the palace of the notoriously messy Snow White. Late to arrive to the party is the perpetually neat Cinderella who has run away from home after becoming fed up with being treated like a maid by her stepmother. With no where else to turn, the two total opposites decide to move in together! What could go wrong?

Royalties: $50.00 per performance.

Cast Size: 8 with extras possible.

Running Time: Approximately 45 minutes.

NOW AVAILABLE!!!

Eager to escape the clutches of the Big Bad Wolf once and for all, the Three Little Pigs build a time machine and travel back in time 150 million years to the Jurassic era where they quickly discover they have problems much bigger than the Big Bad Wolf. Much, much, much bigger!!!

Royalties $35.00 per performance.

Cast Size: 6+ extras with flexible M-F roles.

Running Time: Approximately 30 minutes.

NOW AVAILABLE!!!

Dr. Victor "Vickie" Frankenstein has just inherited his grandfather's castle in foggy Transylvania...but what secrets lie in the ultra-secret, sub-terrainian laboratory located beneath the castle??? It's a little bit monster story and a little bit Rock and Roll!

Royalties $50.00 per performance.

Cast Size: 16. 8 principle roles, 8+ Extras possible.

Running Time: Approximately one hour.

11683865R00051

Printed in Great Britain
by Amazon